BOOK 4

ALL ABOUT GARDEN TREES

JOHN BRADSHAW'S
COMPLETE GUIDE TO
BETTER GARDENING
IN SIXTEEN VOLUMES

"Copyright Owners"

LELAND PUBLISHING COMPANY

NEW YORK • BUFFALO • TORONTO

Year of Publication 1961

©

Printed in U.S.A.

TABLE OF CONTENTS

INTRODUCTION

SHADE TREES

FLOWERING SHADE TREES

FRUIT TREES

Courtesy of McConnell Nurseries

**Trees blend the house and surrounding landscape together
as if they had existed for many years**

INTRODUCTION

There is no greater natural asset to property than trees, they add beauty, form windbreaks, give shade, privacy and an extensive variety of colour, and incidentally add value to your home.

Trees serve to blend the house and the surrounding landscape together as if they had existed for many years, they also pro-vide an effective background to the home. The various shapes of the individual trees create a great deal of the attractiveness and the beauty found in a garden. Trees provide shade on the hot Summer days, and colour the year round. It would be impossible to imagine a garden without at least three or four shade, flowering or fruit trees.

Courtesy of A. B. Morse Co.

A well placed shade tree can be a source of year-round enjoyment

Courtesy of Ontario Horticultural Society

This is what happens when the taller trees are not kept to the sides and rear of the property

In selecting suitable locations for various trees, the best plan is to keep the taller ones to the sides and rear of the property. It's a good plan to look out through the windows when selecting choice locations for trees. By doing this, you will be able to choose planting sites that will not only provide garden beauty, but also frame or add to the view as seen from indoors.

Plan before you plant—A well placed shade tree in a garden can be a source of year around enjoyment, not only for the home owner and family, but for those who visit or just pass by. On the other hand, trees planted in the wrong spots end up as nothing but a nuisance.

Before planting study carefully the pros and cons of the trees in which you are interested. What are the rooting and branching habits, how tall will it be at maturity, is

Before planting find out the rooting and branching habits of a tree

Courtesy of New Brunswick Dept. of Travel

Courtesy of the City of Winnipeg

The hot summer sun can be very uncomfortable without adequate shade

it able to stand up to the weather, smog, insects and diseases? Your final choice must be trees you can manage within your particular circumstances. It is obvious the gardener with an average sized lot will be restricted to trees fairly small in size, easily pruned and otherwise maintained.

Beware of the pitfalls. A great favourite, the weeping willow, eventually develops a root system larger than the average house, so don't plant one on the corner of your house or adjacent to a drainage system!

It may be repetitious, but please watch those hydro and telephone wires, your house and neighbours' property when planting taller trees, it can be very disappointing to have branches lopped off or even the whole tree removed.

A blue spruce, or a fast growing pine, planted in front of windows will soon force you to remove it. "Think before you plant", is a good resolution for the trees.

Air conditioning with shade trees — The hot Summer sun can be very uncomfortable without adequate shade on your property. The answer is in placing shade trees in a position — giving the utmost protection from the sun. Plant the trees at some distance of the place you want shaded, slightly north of due west. If you plant the tree, or trees, right over the spot, the shade will fall to the east of it in the afternoon.

The hottest part of the Summer day is usually in the mid and late afternoon, when the sun's rays slant considerably. To com-

Courtesy of Nova Scotia Dept. of Travel

Beware the weeping willow on the small property

bat this, plant far enough to the west so the tree will intercept the slanted rays and the shade fall on the desired area.

For shade directly over outdoor living areas at mid-day, the tree should be planted at the edge of the area, but not where an outdoor fireplace will scorch leaves on the lower branches.

The same rules hold true for shade on a terrace or patio. If the terrace is on the east side of the house only the directly overhead sun needs to be screened off because the house will shade the terrace in the afternoon. In this case the shade tree can be right beside the patio or terrace to guard against the mid-day sun. But if the patio is on the west side of the house, two trees may be needed, one at some distance to the west to block the hot afternoon sun and one close to the patio to intercept the sun's rays at mid-day and up to the middle of the afternoon.

Courtesy of Mr. G. Hamilton

On a hot summer day shade can mean the difference between comfort and discomfort

Shade trees can make a difference of 4 to 10 degrees in the temperature of the outdoor living area. This can mean the difference on a hot Summer day between comfort and discomfort. Correctly located shade trees will also eliminate the harsh glare of the sun.

These suggestions for locating shade trees can also be used to make various rooms inside the house more comfortable by shading the wall of the house and one or more windows from the hot afternoon sun.

How to plant a shade tree — Every Spring the nurseryman gets a lot of blame he doesn't deserve when a shade or flowering tree fails to grow. Most failures along this line are due to poor planting methods by the home gardener.

Is it worth taking the time to plant a tree

Courtesy of the Dept. of Travel, New Brunswick

Homes surrounded by trees sell faster at 15% to 20% higher prices.

correctly? The answer is a loud and resounding "yes".

Your trees are an important physical and financial asset. It's a proven fact that homes surrounded by good trees sell faster and at 15 to 20 percent higher prices.

Proper planting of a tree doesn't mean just digging a hole, placing the tree in it and filling up that hole with soil. If possible, it will pay you to go out to the nursery or garden center and pick your own tree, bring it directly home and plant it. While at the garden center you can obtain the ingredients you don't have at home which are necessary to get the tree off to a good start. These include a good soil mixture to replace the soil removed when digging the planting hole, some peat moss, a bag of complete plant food or fertilizer, and a wooden stake to hold the tree upright.

Before you leave the nursery or garden center make sure that the roots are com-

Courtesy of the Dept. of Travel, New Brunswick

**More trees fail to grow because the roots are allowed to dry out
before planting than any other cause**

pletely covered with damp burlap so they won't dry out in the sun and wind on the way home. More trees fail to grow because the roots are allowed to dry out before planting than any other cause. Trees are always shipped balled and burlapped. Do not remove the burlap but plant as soon as possible after you bring the tree home from the nursery, or it is delivered to your house. This could mean ordering the planting materials mentioned before, several days ahead of the expected arrival of the tree.

If you *cannot* plant right away then heel the tree out in the garden until you can. Heeling-in simply means the storing of a dormant plant, like a tree, in a trench until conditions are favourable for planting. Just dig a trench twelve to fifteen inches deep making one side vertical and one side a long slope. Across the slope lay the tree with the roots extending to the bottom of the trench and facing the vertical side. Before heeling-in newly received trees and shrubs be sure to remove all packing material. Fill in the whole trench, gradually adding soil and firming it around the roots to prevent air spaces.

Nursery stock can be left in such a trench for as long as two or three weeks without harm but the sooner you can plant the better.

When it comes to the actual planting, make sure you dig a hole large enough to accommodate the roots without cramping them. The soil you remove should be discarded and replaced with a soil mixture con-

Courtesy of Siebenthaler Nursery

Good drainage is essential for shade trees such as the Moraine Ash

Right and wrong methods of removing small branches

The final cut in the removal of a limb should be made as close as possible to the trunk

sisting of three parts good garden loam, two parts peat moss and one part coarse sand. In the bottom of the hole, place two handfuls of a complete plant food or fertilizer and cover this with two inches of the soil mixture. Then make a mound of soil in the bottom of the hole to bring the soil level up to planting depth. The tree should be planted about an inch deeper than the planting depth at the nursery. This is the time also to put the stake for the tree in place. By doing this now you will avoid damaging the roots later on.

Next add three or four inches of the soil mixture and thoroughly tramp or firm this around the roots so there will be no air spaces. Experience shows you can do this best by stamping with your feet right in the hole. But don't try to firm the soil into brick. Add another two or three inches of soil and firm again. Then fill the hole with water and let this drain completely away before adding the remainder of the soil.

The tree is going to require plenty of water so leave a saucer-shaped depression around the trunk of the tree for watering

purposes. It won't hurt to water the tree every day for the first two or three months but whatever you do, don't let the roots dry out.

A piece of an old rubber tire tube makes an excellent way of tying the tree to the stake. In making this tie, be sure that you don't have it so tight that it will girdle the tree as it grows.

Good drainage is essential — Many shade trees fail to grow well in the home garden because of poor drainage. For this reason, homeowners frequently have difficulty in establishing trees in areas where the soil consists largely of heavy clay subsoil turned up in the building of their houses.

Lightening heavy clay soil around a tree's root zone by the addition of peat moss, material from the home compost heap, or other forms of humus at planting time may not help the drainage problem. In some cases it can make matters worse. If the water cannot penetrate the surrounding clay, it may gather around the tree's roots and be

36 hours. If water remains in the hole at the end of that time without replenishment from rain or other sources, then the drainage is unsatisfactory.

Here are several things to remedy this situation. Perhaps the surface of the ground can be regraded to encourage better runoff. Or, if there is a lower surface level nearby, drain tiles can be laid to carry water from the bottom of the planting hole to a lower spot where it will run away. This, of course requires digging a trench to lay the drain tile—a difficult job if the distance is great. Another method, which may be better in some instances, is to dig the planting hole somewhat deeper than necessary to accommodate the roots and fill the bottom with a generous layer of coarse gravel. This will allow room for water to stand where it will not touch the tree roots. If surface runoff is slow, soil should be mounded around the base of the tree to keep water from gathering there. And sometimes it is better to fill the hole with the same dirt that was taken out so as not to encourage standing water in the tree's root zone.

Protect your trees from the onslaught of the bulldozer

trapped there. This is like planting a tree in a bucket of water, and few trees will survive such treatment.

A good way to test for bad drainage is to dig a hole about 18 inches deep in the spot where you are planning to plant a tree. Fill the hole with water and allow it to stand for

Don't apply 2,4-D on a windy day

Proper way to apply 2,4-D

Feeding shade and fruit trees — Very few home gardeners ever bother to feed their trees, they just plant them and expect them to grow well for the rest of their life. This is a fallacy because there is not an inexhaustible supply of plant food in the soil. Each year as the roots of the trees take up the food in soluble form, the amount of plant food is diminished, never to be replaced unless you do it.

What will happen if you give a mature tree a feeding? If it hasn't been fed for some time it will usually grow two to three feet the first year after feeding! One of the very best ways of keeping insect pests and diseases to a minimum is to feed your shade and fruit trees regularly.

Feeding time is either in the month of April or during October.

"For small trees" the best method is to broadcast a complete fertilizer in a circle on the ground beneath the outer spread of the branches.

"To feed bigger trees" you need to drill a series of holes beneath the outer spread of branches. Make the holes 2 inches in diameter, 18 inches deep and 18 inches apart. Feeding a larger tree this way is quite a job but there are no halfway measures. All too often, home gardeners try to get by with a few holes in the sod which means that very few of the feeding roots get correct nourishment.

Most trees have a root system at least as wide as their branch spread, with the majority of the feeding roots within a circle on or just beyond the drip line. What's a drip line? It's the circle described by the arching branches of the trees. Drill the holes in staggered fashion. Take some sand or dry soil and mix it half and half with the complete fertilizer and fill up the holes.

There is a new complete fertilizer in a stick form now on the market which is much

In removing large limbs, the first cut should be made a couple of feet from the trunk

easier to handle than having to mix the fertilizer with sand or dry soil and put it in the holes. In using this new stick fertilizer you drop one in each hole and your work is finished. The holes don't need to be nearly so large either.

Fruit trees also need an annual feeding. This is usually done by the broadcast method. In other words you scatter the fertilizer in a wide band around the trees at the drip line. Make a start about half way between the trunk and the end of the limbs and extend about the same distance beyond the ends of the limbs.

Fertilizing trees in the lawn — If the fruit or other trees are planted as lawn specimens, make sure the grass is dry before applying the fertilizer or some burning of the grass can take place. It's also a wise plan to sweep the lawn with a broom or the back of a rake to knock any lumps of fertilizer off the grass. Get out the hose and thoroughly soak the fertilizer into the ground.

In feeding shade trees, make sure you put the holes just underneath or beyond the dripline

Fruit trees — Mature apple trees 15 years or older should be fed 10 to 12 lbs of fertilizer per tree. 6 to 8 lbs is required by the average 10 year old peach tree. Plums, pears and cherries will require less, say 5 to 6 lbs per tree.

Raising the soil level around trees— How high can soil be raised around a tree without injuring it? The answer to this lies in the type of the soil surrounding the tree. Where the soil is light and well drained, the level of the soil around the tree can be raised as much as a foot with very little injury or harm. On the other hand, in heavy clay and not well drained soil, raising the grade as little as six inches can cause injury. This really has the effect of strangling the tree.

If you wish to get a satisfactory slope for the lawn, and this means raising the existing level of soil around a tree or trees, your only answer is to build a loose stone or brick wall around the trunk which will allow air and moisture to reach the roots. Such a wall is often called a "well", and its diameter should be four times the diameter of the trunk. For instance, if the tree trunk is 2 feet in diameter, then that of the well should be 8 feet. Any well that needs to be more than 2 feet deep will need tile drains running out horizontally from the bottom. Be sure you don't narrow the well at the top when building it or you will have difficulty each year cleaning out leaves and other debris.

Metal tree guards — The only sure way of protecting shade, fruit and flowering trees when they're small is to use metal tree guards. These will not only serve to protect the trees from rabbit or mice injuries, but will give good protection from mower damage during the Summer months.

These metal tree guards should be extended into the ground for at least 2 inches. This will help to deter rodents from burrowing down under the wire guard. Unfortunately, some of them get over-ambitious and do get underneath the guard. You can prevent this by placing crushed stones, cinders or coarse gravel around the base of the tree. Make this layer 1½ to 2 inches deep.

Be sure and practise clean cultivation by keeping grass or straw mulch away from these tree guards. This will go a long way to discouraging the mice from burrowing into the mulch and finally getting at the bark of the tree and girdling it.

Tree wounds and their treatment — Most persons don't realize it's just as easy to injure a tree trunk or a branch as it is a human being. Any wounds or cuts on a tree need the same prompt treatment to prevent infection by disease and to stop insect pests from gaining an easy entry into the tree. In giving the tree the right treatment it may be necessary to be quite ruthless. Jagged breaks or abrasions should first of all be cut clean with a sharp knife or saw. It's important to clear away all dead or diseased portions of the wood or bark. Often this requires cutting off branches or limbs, or cutting out diseased portions.

As a general rule (except for the most minor cuts or breaks) it pays to call in a reliable and recognized tree expert.

Wounds should be sterilized, especially

A layer of gravel around the tree will prevent damage by the lawnmower

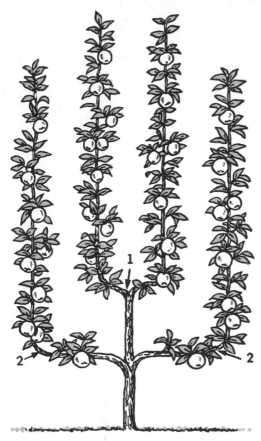

**Dwarf Fruit Trees can be trained like
grape-vine (espalier)**

older ones which have become infected.

Use a copper sulphate solution mixed in the proportion of 1 lb. of copper sulphate to 3 gallons of water. Then protect and waterproof with one of the tree emulsions or paints that are commercially available for this purpose.

Getting rid of tree stumps — Tree stumps have the habit of turning up in the strangest places. They always seem to be present in the middle of the garden, lawn or in the middle of a field where we have to go around them. Getting rid of such a stump usually takes a lot of work and it can be seldom done quickly.

One of the easiest solutions, if the stump is in the middle of the garden or along the side, is to dress it up by placing a flower box or container on top. Such a box or container would have to be at least 8 inches deep and will need filling with a good soil mixture to within 1 inch of the top. The space at the top is left to permit adequate watering. You can either make up your own soil mixture consisting of three parts good top soil, one part humus, and one part sand, or you can buy one of the commercially prepared soils at your nearby nursery or garden center. When you prepare your own soil mixture, be sure and add a tablespoonful of complete fertilizer for each quart of soil used.

The box could be painted white or a colour that would match the colour scheme of your house or garage. Painting the stump is not advised, as it looks much better if it's left in its natural state. A good looking combination of flowers for such a flower box could consist of three or four either pink or red geraniums, two or three White Satin petunias, and some trailing blue lobelia. There are two kinds of lobelia usually sold, so be sure and ask for the trailing kind. They will trail down over the sides of the box and in combination with the generaniums and petunias make a most attractive picture.

Removing tree stumps with a chemical—A garden problem which creates a great deal of difficulty for many city and town gardeners is the removal of a tree stump where it is impossible to use a bulldozer or any heavy machinery. Spring is the time to do something about it.

The first step is to bore a vertical hole, one and a half inches in diameter and eighteen inches deep in the center of the stump. In it pour one and a half ounces of salt peter, which is uusally available at the corner drug store. Fill the remainder of the hole with water and plug tightly. Next Spring remove the plug and pour ten

Dwarf apples and pears can be trained along a fence in espalier fashion

ounces of coal oil into the hole and ignite. You will find the stump will smoulder away even to the ends of the roots without blazing, and nothing but ashes will be left.

What to do with leaves—The smell of burning leaves seems to be a wonderful perfume to some people. But to many more it means a terrible waste of one of nature's most abundant fertilizers. The best plan of course is to place the leaves that fall on your property into your own compost heap. If that is not possible please don't burn them but see the leaves are made available either to the city or to a neighbour who could use them.

The compost box is a must for any garden

"Every garden should have its own compost heap." In it is broken down into humus a host of waste materials including grass cuttings, leaves (except oak), vegetables, vines, flower stalks and weeds. From the house come citrus fruit peel, discarded vegetable leaves such as lettuce, cabbage and cauliflower, potato peelings, carrots, turnips, parsnips, beets etc. In addition, you can also add faded flowers and hulls from strawberries; in fact, any leafy vegetable and flower refuse.

You may ask, "Why go to all this trouble? Just pop it into the garbage and forget about it." But this is breaking one of the fundamental laws of conservation. In the production of flowers, leaves, trunks and branches, fruits and vegetables, plant food and other material is taken from the soil and also the soil's vital supply of humus is used up. Unless this is replaced the soil becomes gradually poorer and eventually almost useless. That's the story of the agriculture of many past civilizations. When the soil goes, so does the power and influence of a nation and its standard of living.

The best way of keeping up a good

supply of humus in the soil is to add to it each year valuable humus manufactured in the home compost heap. Read also Book I of this series for the full story on compost heaps.

Perhaps the easiest way of making one is to use cement blocks. A good average size for most gardens would be six feet long and four feet wide. The blocks can be bought and added to the compost box as it is filled. Down through the middle of the four corner blocks drive iron pipes or stakes to hold the box reasonably rigid.

Some people have used scrap lumber and even snow fences to good advantage, others swear by plaster lathes. The kind of siding you use to enclose the material really doesn't matter so long as it keeps the heap neat and tidy.

In using the cement blocks put the first rectangular layer in place. Leave one end open at the start so you can dump the material in easily. As you add the material, tramp it down until you have a layer six inches deep. Soak it with water. Now do the whole process again until you have another six inch layer. Again soak with water. Additional cement blocks may be added as needed.

The composting of leaves and other leafy material from the garden can be speeded up by turning the material every two days and seeing that the moisture content remains high. This can be an advantage early in the gardening season, because the humus so created can be used in a number of ways around the garden. However, in the case of leaves in the Fall, the gardening season is just about at an end, making speed unnecessary. The leaves can be added to the compost heap as outlined above, and by the time Spring arrives, they will have decomposed into the desired form of humus.

Think before you cut down any tree

—During the outward growth of cities and towns, ground is greedily gobbled up for housing and ever growing industry. Among the victims of this expansion are our trees.

It isn't often nowadays that we can drive around newly forming suburbs and see that the trees have been spared. Most have been ruthlessly swept away. Yet their inspiring majesty, form and dignity takes years to formulate. The beauty of our wooded developments is so obvious when compared to those whose lots have been denuded.

What chance has a one hundred year old tree against a bulldozer? When we consider that trees are a part of our heritage and must be cherished, the question arises as to the awareness of our real estate sub-dividers to their responsibilities not only to the present, but to the future.

In all fairness the home buyer should be prepared to pay just a little more for his house in order to preserve the trees standing on the lot. The extra cost is so very low in comparison to the money needed to replant the property with suitable trees that it is hard to imagine anyone quibbling.

Subdividers would be well advised to retain the services of a reliable firm of tree experts before they commit a new building area to the onslaught of the bulldozer.

Many other subdivisions have been built through necessity on farm land denuded of trees by previous generations. Here we have the opportunity to do ourselves and the future generations a real service by replanting the trees. We say future generations because in many cases the trees we plant will not reach anywhere near maturity in our lifetime.

Immediate shade can be secured by moving into place a large-sized tree. What is the best size for this purpose? Tree experts regard one with a trunk from 4 to 6

Courtesy of A. B. Morse Co.

Immediate beauty and shade can be secured by moving into place a large size tree

inches in diameter and 18 to 20 feet in height as the ideal size for this purpose. Moving such trees will cost money, but not as much as you might think. Especially when you consider the extra value it will add to the property. No other kind of landscaping will add so much value for money spent. Costs will vary depending where you live, but make sure you are doing business with the most reliable and experienced firm possible. You are entitled to insist on a guarantee (look with distrust on any firm that refuses to give a guarantee). The usual guarantee states that if the tree dies within six months, provided it has been given reasonable care, it will be replaced at half the original cost. So the best insurance against loss of a tree is to make sure that you have a reliable firm of tree experts do the job.

Beware of the type of firm offering to sell you trees from the woods and forests at bargain rates. These almost invariably have the wrong root systems for moving purposes. Trees grown in the nursery originally were root pruned a number of times and will have developed a dense compact mass of roots confined within a small area.

TREE WEEDS

Certain extremely fast-growing trees such as the Weeping Willow, Lombardy, and Carolina Poplars, Manitoba Maple and the Chinese Elm are what we call tree weeds. It's true that they grow rapidly and provide quick shade, but they have many faults.

A **Weeping Willow** is entirely too large a tree for the average garden. Under good growing conditions it will fill the average lot 20 years after planting. Its roots will extend out as much as 200 feet to break up tile drains. The damage done would be exactly the same as if you had taken a sledge hammer and smashed them to pieces.

Lombardy and Carolina Poplars reach maturity around 18 years of age and then gradually die over a period of time. They are soft wooded, and particularly susceptible to ice and wind storms.

Manitoba Maple is also a great tree for breaking up tile drains, and its seeds in the early spring create considerable mess. One

Courtesy of Kelly Bros., Dansville, N.Y.
Lombardy Popular

recommended that any of these trees be planted unless exceptional circumstances demand a quick cover for a particularly bad eyesore.

Weeping Willow
Courtesy of Kelly Bros., Dansville, N.Y.

Courtesy of Kelly Bros., Dansville, N.Y.
Chinese Elm

heavy wind or ice storm can wreck the entire tree.

Chinese Elm is another quick growing tree which is easily damaged by wind and ice storms. Its roots will go out for long distances on all sides to rob the surrounding garden of plant food.

In view of their many faults, it is not

RECOMMENDED SHADE TREES

Reliable fast growing shade trees — Twenty years ago, it was almost impossible to recommend a fast growing shade tree that didn't have so many faults that it was hardly worth planting. Today nurserymen have developed quite a number of trees that not only grow quickly but have few faults. Most of them will grow anywhere from 3 to 5 feet in a year once they become established in your garden and it isn't long before you have a satisfactory tree large enough to add beauty, dignity and shade to the garden.

Moraine Locust — Is one of the best of the newest shade trees to be introduced during the past ten years. Locust trees are native to the North Eastern part of the continent and normally should make excellent shade trees for our gardens, but the big trouble with locust trees until now has been the ugly thorns which protrude from the branches. Unsightly seed pods were also a nuisance because they had to be gathered up in the Fall or Winter. The new Moraine Locust trees produce neither thorns nor seed pods yet they grow more rapidly than the common type of locust, and have built-in disease resistance.

This tree grows at the rate of 3 to 5 feet per year which means that under good growing conditions it should reach 25 feet in height in about ten years, considerably faster than the average shade tree will do.

The Moraine Locust is a round-shaped tree when young but grows tall and vase-shaped as it gets older. Now that our beautiful elms are seriously threatened by the Dutch Elm Tree Disease, we can take a certain amount of comfort in the fact that the Moraine Locust makes a very satisfactory substitute. The lower branches tend to self

Courtesy of Kelly Bros., Dansville, N.Y.
Moraine Locust

prune as the top of the tree grows wider. This makes it a practical choice for narrow street plantings as sufficient clearance can be maintained for any type of traffic. Like the common forms of Locusts this tree is tolerant of smoke, soot and dust, making it a practical shade tree for city conditions.

Because of the vase-shaped form of the mature tree and the fine lacy foliage, enough sunlight filters through to permit

Courtesy of Kelly Bros., Dansville, N.Y.
**Moraine Locust is a worthy substitute
for the American Elm**

"Shademaster Locust" — The new tree with all the better qualities. Quick growth, strong and straight, no leaf raking in the fall, free from disease and insects, drought resistant

good growth of lawn grasses. The foliage is dark green and the leaves are lace-like.

Soil doesn't seem to matter too much for these new locusts. They will produce good growth whether your soil is heavy or light but like all other trees will grow much better if they get sufficient food and good moisture conditions.

The ice storms in some areas are a factor in choosing shade trees for the garden. Such storms will be no problem for the Moraine Locust because it is a hardwood with branches that bend easily under heavy strain of wind, snow and ice.

If you have a large lawn, say a half to an acre in size, then you could plant one as a

The Pink Horsechestnut is an excellent flowering and shade tree

specimen tree in the lawn. If not, plant to the side or the rear of the property to form a background for the whole garden.

Whatever you do, don't plant the Moraine Locust below overhead wires. If you do, you will soon have some butchering to do once it reaches the height of the wires. Remember this tree will grow 40 feet high when it reaches maturity.

The falling leaves present little or no problem as they crumple quickly making

raking unnecessary and at the same time the soil gets back some valuable humus.

You can get an idea of the value of this fine new tree when you realize that it is patented and the "Moraine" trade mark is protected by law both in Canada and the United States.

Moraine Ash — Don't confuse this tree with the ordinary ash, as special breeding and selection have eliminated all the unde-

By Malak, Courtesy of the Bulb Growers Assoc. of Holland

A standard apple tree makes a fine flowering tree in the garden

sirable features, and so it's ideal for lawn or street planting. You will be most impressed with its attractive symmetrical shape which forms in its early growth and continues into full maturity. It will grow 35 to 40 feet high eventually.

The Moraine Ash bears small, olive green leaves which persist later in the Autumn than those of most ordinary ash trees. When they do fall, they sift through the lawn grasses and so eliminate raking. This fine new tree also features a smooth attractive bark that adds to its cleanliness and desirability.

It's reported hardy in such cold weather areas as Montana and North Dakota. Another point very much in its favour is its adaptability to a wide variety of soil conditions.

The Mountain Ash — The European Mountain Ash is one of the most popular of the smaller shade trees. This very ornamental tree of moderate growth makes an ideal lawn specimen tree. In the Spring, large, flat clusters of white flowers are produced followed by large bunches of flashy orange red berries which darken as the Summer season ends. This is the tree which causes so much comment each year; the tree that never fails to produce a crop of brilliant red berries. These can be a big factor in attracting birds to the garden. The robins in particular find the berries a tasty tidbit. Deep green, clean foliage perfectly compliments the graceful upright growth. Grows to a height of 18 feet to 25 feet, with a maximum spread of 15 feet. The Mountain Ash is not only suitable for planting in gardens, but for street planting also. Can be grown quite near flower beds without damaging nearby flowers or the lawn underneath.

Pin Oak — Most oak trees are slow

Courtesy of Kelly Bros., Dansville, N.Y.

The European Mountain Ash is one of the best of the smaller shade trees

growers, but the stately pin oak is the exception to the rule and is one of the fastest growing of the oak family. The foliage is rich green, deeply cut and becomes a glossy copper colour in the late Fall. It's one of the

The Pin Oak is a fast grower

Courtesy of Kelly Bros., Dansville, N.Y.

Courtesy of Coles Nurseries

The Sunburst Locust is one of the most beautiful shade trees available today

Courtesy of Ontario Agricultural College, Guelph, Ont.

**The lovely Golden Chain Tree is a
show plant all season**

Winter months. The fine green foliage is a joy to behold.

Little Leaf Linden — Here we have an ideal shade tree for the home garden, and one of the very best trees for street planting, as it is able to withstand the fumes, smoke and dust better than most trees. The trees are very long lived, have a dense pyramidal shape, have handsome heart-shaped foliage, and grows to 100 feet.

Weeping Mulberry — One of the finest of the small lawn specimen trees which only grows 6 feet high. It's sometimes called the "umbrella tree" and has long weeping branches which grow up to 5 feet in length. The fruits are tasty and edible and are attractive not only to human beings, but also birds.

**Little Leaf Linden is one of the very best
trees for street planting**

Courtesy of A. B. Morse Co.

few trees that are generally disease and insect free. Everyone likes its symmetrical, pyramidal form. At maturity it stands 30 to 40 feet high.

Pyramidal Oak — This striking vertical oak tree is not listed by every nursery, but the trouble you may have in finding it will be forgotten when you see it growing in your garden. It grows in the same shape as the Lombardy Poplar, but has none of its faults. The Lombardy poplar tends to grow very fast until it is about 20 years of age and then gradually dies away. The Pyramidal Oak on the other hand is more compact, slower growing and lives for a great many years. Once its leaves turn brown in the Fall, they continue to cling to the branch until early the next Spring, giving the tree a most attractive appearance throughout the

European Beech — There is no doubt that the purple-leaved beech is one of the most colourful and beautiful of all shade trees. It is easily grown and long lived, growing 60 to 70 feet at maturity. The leaves come out a deep maroon in the Spring, turn gradually to a dark maroon-purple in the Summer, and in the Fall become a rich purple-brown. Shapely symmetry, growth and richness of colour add that final touch of elegance to the garden. This is not a tree for the very small garden, and even when planted in the larger gardens should be kept to the side or the rear of the property.

Sunburst Thornless Locust — The most spectacular introduction in the past few years as far as ornamental shade trees are concerned is without a doubt the Sunburst Thornless Locust. It is the first new colour in a hardy ornamental shade tree in many years and is another fast growing tree having few, if any, faults. Being hardwood

Courtesy of McConnell Nurseries, Pt. Burwell, Ont.

Each branch of the Sunburst Locust is a glowing gold color all season long

Purple Leaved Beech is easily grown and is long-lived

Courtesy of Kelly Bros., Dansville, N.Y.

it is much better for planting in the garden than willows, poplars, Manitoba maples; these soft-wooded trees are easily broken down in storms as they do not have the ability to withstand the onslaught of wind and ice.

The brilliant colour and graceful form of the Sunburst Locust combined with its excellent pyramidal branching habit, has already won a whole host of friends and will win many more in the coming years.

The leaves are so small that they do not create a maintenance problem. They are fine enough to fall between the grass plants, thus eliminating the necessity of raking. The tips of the branches are bright golden yellow, shading to bronze at the ends and

Courtesy of Siebenthaler Nurseries

The Moraine Locust will grow 3 to 5 feet a year depending on the soil conditions

Courtesy of A. B. Morse Co.

Schwedleri Maple has beautiful reddish-purple foliage during May and June

appear as if you've taken a paint brush and covered the tips of each branch with a bright gold paint. Having rich green inner foliage, the contrast from the branches make it look like a flowering tree just bursting into bloom.

What's still more important, this fine tree keeps its beautiful appearance all Summer long.

This new Sunburst Thornless Locust has been found to be extremely hardy in test plantings throughout the country! It transplants easily and is adaptable to almost any locality.

While it is a very fast grower, it will not grow out of bounds, and its eventual height at maturity is 30 to 40 feet. It makes an excellent lawn specimen shade tree, because the diameter of the trunk is very small in relation to other trees of similar height.

Home gardeners who plant this tree will find it full of dividends—beautiful, colour-

Courtesy of Ontario Horticultural Association

Shade trees and a lily pond add extra beauty to a garden

Courtesy of Ontario Horticultural Association

Flower borders and trees combine for garden charm

ful, straight growing, shapely, disease and insect resistant, requiring minimum care and a worthy substitute for the stately elm.

Supplies of Sunburst locusts have been limited until recently, but now a good supply is in prospect. For a new tree, it is not expensive and sells for $7 to $8 for a 6 to 8 foot specimen.

Norway Maple — Talk to any nurseryman and he'll tell you that one of the biggest sellers in shade trees is the Norway Maple. It's a stately round headed tree capable of withstanding smoke, soot and other adverse growing conditions. For generations it has been recognized as one of the choicest shade trees. The leaves are dark green and very dense all over the tree. In the Fall they turn a rich yellow and orange to create an impressive sight. It's a fine, long lived and hardy tree. The Norway Maple is very hard wooded and does not break down in wind and ice storms. You'll find it a medium fast growing tree that will add real beauty to your garden. However, in making plans to set one out in your garden, remember that it will eventually grow 50 to 60 feet high and so there is no use locating it underneath public utility wires. If your nurseryman offers you a choice in height take the taller tree. You may pay a dollar or two more for

it but you will get shade much more quickly.

Harlequin Maple—This is a new variegated-leaf Norway Maple. Try and visualize a tree completely covered with variegated silver green leaves. The center of the leaf is a rich green, the outside edge is silver-white. It's a moderately rapidly growing tree which develops a lovely round head. It is a rare tree seldom seen in gardens, yet is per-

Norway Maple withstands adverse growing conditions such as soot and smoke

Courtesy of Kelly Bros., Dansville, N.Y.

fect for shade on the lawn. At maturity it will be approximately 40 feet tall.

Crimson King Maple — Here is a wonderful tree so colourful and beautiful that it deserves a place on every lawn. It also is a Norway Maple which came to this continent some years ago from Europe. Since then it has created the same sensation over here as it did in Europe. Its leaves are a bright purple-maroon giving an effect not unlike a Copper Beech except that the top of the branches and the new growth of leaves are much redder. This colour glistens so brightly and brilliantly in the sunshine, that Crimson King actually gives the impression of being in bloom all Summer long. The trees are extremely hardy and withstand the coldest temperatures.

It grows from 25 to 40 feet in height. Smoke, dust or gases do not have noticeable effects on it, so it will bring your garden colourful beauty for generations to come.

A Crimson King Maple has many uses: it's superb for lawns both large and small, makes a fine tree for street planting and is wonderful when used as a contrast among other trees.

Scarlet Maple (Rubrum) — Here's a shade tree that not only has bright green leaves all Summer long but whose vivid

The rich color of the Copper Beech adds a touch of elegance to any garden

Courtesy of Ontario Agricultural College

Courtesy of Kelly Bros., Dansville, N.Y.

Crimson King Maple keeps its beautiful color from Spring until the leaves fall

Fall colours catch everyone's attention. These colours are rich reds, crimsons, orange and scarlet, and are truly the brightest of any of the autumn colourings. This tall spreading tree prefers a slightly moist location. Height at maturity is 40 to 50 feet.

Sugar Maple (Saccharum) — Don't confuse the Sugar Maple with the Silver Maple whose Latin name is almost the same. Saccharinum is the botanical name of the Silver Maple. While the Silver Maple is a fast growing tree it's also soft-wooded and breaks down easily in ice and snow storms and so is not recommended for home garden planting. On the other hand, the

Courtesy of Kelly Bros., Dansville, N.Y.

A Sugar Maple is a fine rather slow growing tree

Courtesy of Kelly Bros., Dansville, N.Y.

Japanese Red Maple is a rare and colorful dwarf tree

Sugar Maple is a fine tree although it's rather slow growing. You'll discover it to be an excellent shade tree of upright dense growth having excellent green leaves which turn to bright yellow and red in the Fall. This is the tree which can be tapped later in its lifetime for the sweet sap which boils down to make maple syrup. It's perfectly hardy, well branched, developing into one of the finest trees. Maturity height is 40 to 60 feet.

Schwedler Maple — During the past two decades the Schwedler Maple has become a very popular shade tree. In the early Summer it has reddish purple foliage which changes to green towards the end of June. This maple is hard wooded and has a good branching habit. It needs to be planted to the sides or rear of the property as it grows 30 to 50 feet in height.

Japanese Red Maple — This is a rare and colourful dwarf tree growing approxi-

mately 6 feet, sometimes used as a small shrub. Because of its slow growth it makes an excellent specimen tree or shrub for the lawn. Its foliage is never dense enough to harm the lawn and its brilliant crimson foliage never fails to attract attention. Having leaves blood red in colour there's nothing better for contrasting among the evergreens in the foundation planting or in the shrub border. The Japanese Maple does best when planted in full sun but will tolerate moderate shade. Under shady conditions the crimson colour is not nearly so pronounced.

White Birch — One of the best ways of using the beautiful white silver birch trees around the garden, is to plant them in clumps of three. Granted, a single tree is also very attractive, but a clump of three seems to add much more charm to the garden. The growth of the white birch is gracefully upright. Even in the Winter the delicate branches make a lovely silhouette against the drab colours of the other trees in the background.

It's best not to start with trees that are too large. If well fed and watered, birches are fast growers, considering the fact that they're a hardwood. Eventually they'll grow 35 to 40 feet in height, so don't plant them underneath or close to public utility wires.

Don't be disappointed if the bark of your birch trees is not always white, because often they do not reach this colour until they are about four years old. At this time a chemical change takes place enabling the bark to become white.

You can create some wonderful effects in your garden, by placing a flower bed around a clump of birches.

In all too many cases, most people use them merely as a lawn specimen. This is a mistake, because by placing a large flower

Courtesy of Kelly Bros., Dansville, N.Y.

Wonderful effects can be created by placing a flower bed around a clump of birches

A Cut-Leaved Weeping Birch is one of our most graceful shade trees

Courtesy of McConnell Nurseries, Pt. Burwell, Ont.

bed at the base of the clump of these white silver birches your garden can come alive with a beauty not usually seen in the garden world.

Someone has said that white birches and daffodils were created for each other. You will know this statement to be true if you plant a big bed of Dutch Master or one of the other newer and large-flowered trumpet daffodils around the base of the trees. The bright golden yellow of the flowers makes a truly delightful contrast from the delicate white bark of the birches. An even more dramatic effect can be created with the soft pastel pinks and apricots of the new Pink Daffodils. Wild Rose and Pink Beauty are excellent for this purpose. The daffodils could be interplanted with a soft pink tulip like Rosy Wings to prolong the early Spring flowering season.

Once these Spring flowering bulbs have faded, they can be replaced with one of the newer petunias such as the delightful salmon-coloured Maytime or the free

Courtesy of Princeton Nurseries, Princeton, N.J.

The new Moraine Ash makes an excellent lawn specimen tree

The stately Birch in delightful combination with daffodils

flowering Pink or Peach Satin.

As the birch trees grow larger, tuberous begonias can also be planted in the bed around the base. The partially shaded conditions created by the branches and foliage will give the begonias the shade they need in order to grow well. Again the soft pinks and the golden yellow coloured varieties of begonias will create a breathtaking garden scene.

For larger gardens and after the silver birches have been growing for several years, you could plant some bushes of the golden forsythia around the base and again create a wonderful contrast between the buttercup yellow of the forsythia and the white of the birches.

Cut leaved Weeping Birch — There is no doubt that this spectacular tree is unsurpassed by any other tree for the beauty and the grace of its drooping branches, silvery-white bark and delicately cut foliage. It will make a most splendid

Courtesy of Kelly Bros., Dansville, N.Y.

A Weeping Birch needs lots of room, so keep it some distance away from the house or other buildings

specimen tree that will add considerably to the value and beauty of your property. Even in Winter, without foliage the delicate weeping branches create a lovely picture. It is not too particular as to soil, but prefers a moist location and sunny spot in the garden. In planting always cut back the branches (except the leader) at least one third. As with any tree, never expose the roots to the sun or wind while planting. Spring planting is the best for these fine trees. About the only thing that could be said which is not in their favour is the fact that they are often attacked by the leaf miner and other injurious insects. Dusting or spraying several times during the gardening season with an all-purpose insecticide and fungicide will keep these under control.

FLOWERING SHADE TREES

Nothing will add more beauty, charm and distinctiveness to any garden, large or small, than the flowering shade trees. Many of them seem to be especially designed for

A Forsythia and a White Birch make a good combination in the garden

Courtesy of Kelly Bros., Dansville, N.Y.

Courtesy of The Augustine Elm Association

Augustine Ascending Elm

the small garden, because they don't grow very tall or cover a large area at maturity. Their average height is 15 feet.

The beautiful display of bloom in early or late Spring followed closely by fine foliage gives these trees a big advantage over the non-flowering type. Many of the low growing flowering shade trees are excellent lawn specimen trees. One or more flowering shade trees should be among the first things planted in the garden.

RECOMMENDED VARIETIES

Flowering Crab Apple — A flowering crab apple tree in full bloom is a joy to behold in any garden. One or more of these delightful trees are a must for even the smallest garden. After the flowers fade they remain an attractive shade tree with bronze-coloured foliage. Finally, as Summer fades, they are covered with attractive fruits, many of which are edible. Another important point in their favour, is that they can be

Courtesy of Kelly Bros., Dansville, N.Y.

The Almey Crab will enrich your garden with masses of brilliant fiery-crimson flowers

grown either as a comparatively low grow-ing tree or as a tall shrub.

A check through your nursery catalogue will show that the trees are very inexpen-sive. There isn't a flowering tree that is any hardier or easier to grow. A colour range of the flowers is truly out of this world ranging from whites through brilliant pinks to ox-blood red and wine-purple. Most varieties of flowering crab apples grow to a maxi-mum height of 15 or so feet if left unpruned, but you can keep them to any height by hard pruning. Used as shrubs, they can be kept low-growing to fit the style of the ranch style homes being built today. Crab apples can be safely planted under or close to utility lines because of their low height at maturity.

When ordering crab apples from the nursery, be sure to specify whether you want the tree or the shrub form.

They do not require any special type of soil and will grow well in ordinary garden

Flowering trees, shrubs and tulips create a charming scene

Courtesy of Ontario Agricultural College

Courtesy of Patmore Nurseries, Brandon, Manitoba

Crab apples are extremely hardy and will survive sub-zero temperatures

Horticultural Experimental Station, Vineland,, Ont.

A Japanese Cherry makes a fine flowering tree where temperatures seldom fall below zero

earth. The method of planting is exactly the same as for any shade tree.

Almey Crab — There is no doubt that the Almey crab is one of the most beautiful of all the flowering crab apples. Your garden will be enriched by masses of huge flowers which are brilliant fiery crimson in colour. White markings at the base of each petal give the effect of a five-sided star. Almey grows 12 to 15 feet in height at maturity. It's a vigorous grower and soon attains just the right size for the modern ranch style home, very often blooming the first year after planting. It's perfectly hardy even in the coldest sections and thrives in full sunshine or partial shade. The brilliantly coloured scarlet fruits hang on to the branches long after the leaves have dropped and provide late Fall colour for the garden.

Strathmore Crab Tree — Is a new type of pyramidal flowering crab which features glorious blossoms and handsome foliage. In early Spring you will enjoy its masses of rosy pink blossoms that literally cover the tree from top to bottom. When not in bloom the naturally ascending branches are covered with large, reddish bronze leaves that in the Fall turn to shades of brilliant orange and scarlet, accented with hundreds of

miniature apples. Strathmore grows 10 to 15 feet tall in a slim symmetrical column, tapering to a point at the top. Trees are perfectly hardy and have withstood 20° below zero and still blossomed with abundance.

Dolgo Crab Apple — See section on Fruit Trees for description.

Aldenhamensis — Wine purple red flowers, are semi-double. The foliage is a

Crab Apples can either be grown in the tree or shrub form

Courtesy of Kelly Bros., Dansville, N.Y.

bronze colour. Fruit is purple about ¾ of an inch in diameter.

Amisk — Early flowering with very ornamental fruit (not good for cooking). Flower is an amaranth pink with darker veins. Small rosehip-like-fruits are just as beautiful as the flowers, lasting late into the Fall.

Geneva — A dual purpose variety which bears large dark red bloom followed by lovely large dark red apples (about 1½″ in diameter). The fruit has dark red flesh, suitable for cooking and jelly.

Makamik — This variety blooms every year when all others have finished. Its colour is a deep rosy red with darker veins, and produces a big crop of flowers every year. Fruits are small, ½ inch in diameter, and coloured an ox-blood red.

Simcoe — Is a lovely rose pink with reddish bronze foliage. Fruits are an attractive bright red and yellow.

Courtesy of Kelly Bros., Dansville, N.Y.

The flowering Strathmore Crab tree is the only crab apple which is pyramidal in form

The Dolgo Crab not only provdies beautiful flowers but very tasty fruits

Courtesy of Patmore Nurseries, Brandon, Manitoba

Sisipuk — Here we have another very late bloomer, thus prolonging the flowering season. The attractive flowers are rose coloured with a white center. The ox-blood red fruits are ¾″ in diameter, hang on all winter, but are not good for cooking.

Van Essenstine — Is one of the best varieties of flowering crab apples. The growth is upright, clean, and the foliage is a glossy, light green in colour. Flowers are a double pink, being a dark pink on the reverse side, and light pink as the petals open on the inside. It is an excellent variety for cut flower purposes, as the bloom keeps well indoors. Hundreds of blooms are produced every year.

FLOWERING CHERRIES

Kwanzan — This is the spectacular flowering cherry that makes such a wonderful show every year around Washington. D.C. Trees bloom a year or two after transplanting, and grow anywhere from 20 to 30 feet tall. Double bright rose-pink flowers completely clothe the branches in early Spring. It's not hardy in all areas, so check with your local nursery or garden club before you buy.

Hisakura is one of the finer dwarf trees, and is the hardiest of all the Japanese flowering cherries. This variety grows 15 feet tall, and makes an especially good lawn specimen tree. The branches are simply smothered with double pink flowers every Spring.

Paul's Scarlet Hawthorn is the old-fashioned flowering tree that our parents knew and loved. This is not surprising because this exceptionally fine flowering tree produces extra large quantities of double, deep-crimson scarlet flowers, having

Courtesy of Kelly Bros., Dansville, N.Y.

Paul's Scarlet Hawthorn

rich green foliage which makes a wonderful background to highlight the flowers. Its long flowering period and attractive appearance after flowering makes this variety one of the best lawn specimen trees. You get extra beauty later in the season when the abundant scarlet fruit appears. This variety thrives in a number of locations, and is a wise choice for small gardens, growing to about 20 feet.

Magnolia — There is little doubt that the magnolias are one of the most elegant of all the flowering trees. Before the leaves appear, the trees are covered with a mass of fragrant, huge tulip-shaped flowers. These are coloured a rosy-white on the inside, and a lively pink colour on the outside. Leathery, deep green, waxy foliage follows the flowers and provides a restful mass of cool green during the remainder of the growing season. They usually start to flower the second year after planting, and will grow well in any soil having good drainage. They are not reliably hardy in the coldest areas, so check before you plant.

Kwanzan is the Flowering Cherry that makes such a wonderful show every year in Washington, D.C.

Courtesy of Kelly Bros., Dansville, N.Y.

By Malak, Courtesy of the Holland Bulb Growers Association

Getting children to pick tulips is a good way of gaining their interest

Courtesy of Ontario Agricultural College

Magnolias are surprisingly hardy

Golden Rain Trees are one of the best medium size flowering trees in cultivation. In mid-summer the whole tree is a cascade of golden bloom. Golden yellow flowers are borne in long chains which create a breath-taking sight when they stir in the breeze. Used as a specimen lawn tree, it will delight both you and your neighbours. This is a 30 footer.

Golden Chain Tree — Here is another dual-purpose tree which can be grown in either shrub or tree form. In June, the bright golden yellow flowers are produced in long hanging clusters, 18 to 20 inches in length, closely resembling the blooms of the wisteria. This fairly rare dwarf tree has green bark and foliage, and usually flowers the first year after planting. It is not hardy in colder areas, so check before you plant. Height is 8 to 10 feet.

Red Bud — This small tree presents a striking picture, with its clusters of rose pink flowers in the Spring. These are followed by large heart-shaped green leaves. It is very effective for group plantings in corners of the garden or the shrub border. A redbud tree and a bed of yellow violas planted at its base are one of the most beautiful sights in the early Spring. Matures between 15 and 20 feet.

Purple-leaf Plum is one of the finest hardy, small flowering trees for the garden. The flowers are blush pink and are borne in great profusion in the Spring. As they fade, the purple leaves break out on the branches, and keep their colour throughout the Summer. The purple leaf plum makes an excellent contrast when planted among or in front of trees having the usual green foliage. It also makes an excellent lawn specimen tree. The maximum height is 15 feet.

The Magnolia is one of the most elegant of all the flowering trees

Courtesy of Kelly Bros., Dansville, N.Y.

Golden Chain Tree needs sheltering from the cold wintry winds

There is hardly a tree which creates a more spectacular show in the garden than the Golden Rain Tree

Red Chestnut — In choosing an attractive shade tree for the garden, one of the trees you cannot afford to overlook is the Red Horsechestnut. Everyone knows the glorious array of white bloom that the ordinary chestnut produces, but just imagine the same tree with red flowers. It's a fairly fast-growing shade tree which is incredibly beautiful when in bloom. Flowering time is May and June and unlike the common chestnut, this tree does not bear nuts and so is very clean. Grows to about 30 feet.

Early beauty in the garden is provided by the Redbud tree

White Flowering Dogwood — This is one of the most beautiful of our native flowering trees. Here is a superb lawn specimen tree for areas where the Winters are not too cold. It grows well in partial shade and is literally covered with large white blossoms early in the Spring. The flowering dogwood has a very long flowering period of anywhere from 3 to 5 weeks. In the Fall it again puts on a magnificent display with the foliage turning to brilliant shades of

By Malak, Courtesy of the Holland Bulb Growers Association

Tall trees help create a woodland setting for the home

Courtesy of Kelly Bros., Dansville, N.Y.

**Where hardy, the White Flowering
Dogwood is extremely beautiful**

Courtesy of Kelly Bros., Dansville, N.Y.

**An exciting spring show of bloom by the
Red Flowering Dogwood**

red, and at the same time the branches are covered with red berries. Trees grow 10 to 12 feet high.

Red Flowering Dogwood — Everyone should know this lovely artistic flowering tree. It produces a great profusion of large rose-red flowers in the Spring, and glossy red berries in the Fall. There are many locations in the garden where it may be planted, not only because of the exquisite red colour of the flowers, fruits and leaves, but because of its attractive and unique branching habit. 12 feet is its mature height.

**Purple Leaved Plum not only produces
beautiful flowers in the Spring but its
leaves are colorful all season long**

Courtesy of Kelly Bros., Dansville, N.Y.

**Standard apple trees are delightful when
in bloom in May**

Courtesy of the Ontario Agricultural College

Courtesy of A. B. Morse Co.

It's hard to beat the flowering crab apple as a lawn specimen tree

Courtesy of Stark Bros., Louisiana, Missouri

Fruit trees reward a little care handsomely with beauty and fruit

FRUIT TREES

Most gardeners would like to have one or two fruit trees, some are even ambitious to have an orchard. In either case fruit trees are a challenge. They reward a little care handsomely — with beauty and fruit.

With fruit trees we emphasize again, think before you plant. If you have a small lot or back yard then your choice should be dwarf trees. With these you can have a bigger variety of different fruits. You must also consider whether you want late or early bearing varieties.

To some, fruit trees are the most interesting of all trees. Children are fascinated watching the day-by-day development of the

fruit — and what is more tempting than a ready-to-be picked rosy apple or pear!

Before buying any variety of fruit tree be sure to check with your nurseryman for what grows best in your locality.

There aren't many gardens where there is room to grow a standard size apple tree. For instance, a mature Northern Spy apple tree will cover a thousand square feet of space. However, the standard varieties of plums, pears, cherries, peaches and apricots can add a great deal of beauty to the garden, and at the same time won't take up too much room.

They will not only provide the garden

with delicious tasting fruits, but you also get two or three weeks of exquisite bloom from them early in the garden season.

Planting — In some advertisements you will see fruit trees listed as "bearing age." Don't be fooled by this. There is absolutely no advantage to planting such trees and in most cases you won't get as good results as if you'd planted trees of the recommended age.

Best planting age for fruit trees

Apple ------------------- 1 or 2 years
Peach ------------------- 1 year
Cherry ------------------- 1 or 2 years
Plum ------------------- 2 years
Pears ------------------- 2 years

How to plant — Fruit trees can be planted with success in either the Spring or Fall. To ensure fruit trees getting off to a good start, the planting hole should be a good size one. A hole 2 feet wide and 2 feet deep is usually the most satisfactory. True enough, you could get away with a hole 15 inches deep and 15 inches across, but the extra depth and width means that the tree will have lots of nourishment not only immediately available, but for several years to come.

Any earth removed from the hole should be discarded in favour of a correctly prepared planting mixture. Commercially prepared soil mixtures can be bought from the nursery or garden center where you purchased your fruit trees or they are avail-

Best planting age for apple trees is one to two years

Courtesy of Stark Bros., Louisiana, Missouri

Courtesy of Stokes Seed Co.

Plant fruit trees to form a backdrop for a flower bed

able from hardware, department stores, and other places where garden supplies are sold.

It's a good plan, if possible, to have the planting holes dug before you go out to the nursery to pick up your trees. Immediately you arrive home, be sure to get them in the ground. More trees and other nursery stock are killed each year because the stock dries out too much before planting. The roots should be kept covered with a piece of wet burlap or some other material until time to set the trees in the hole.

A small mound of soil should be built up in the bottom of the hole on which to place the tree. This is done to eliminate possible air pockets which in turn would allow the roots to dry out, and in many

cases kill the tree. Just before placing the tree in the hole, it should be examined for any damaged or broken roots and these should be removed with a sharp knife or pruning shears. The roots should be spread out evenly to all sides of the hole and then 3 or 4 inches of soil added and then firmed well around the roots. As the soil is filled in, jiggle the tree a little so that all the roots will make contact with the soil. Keep on adding and firming the soil until the hole is half full. Next, fill the hole with water and let this drain away before filling in the remainder of the soil and firming it.

It's true that you could get away without staking most fruit trees, but experience has shown that a stake can be very valuable in keeping the trees straight and upright until

By Malak, courtesy of Bulb Grower's Association of Holland

Start your children early to get them to enjoy gardening

they have had a chance to form roots and so keep themselves in line. Stakes should be put in place before the earth is filled in around the roots. If you try to put a stake in place after the hole has been filled in, you'll very often do quite a bit of damage to the roots.

APPLE TREES

Recommended varieties of apples

Close is by far the earliest apple to ripen and is an annual bearer of good crops. The apples average 2½ inches in diameter and up and are wonderful for cooking. "Close" is a good shipper and does not bruise easily. The fruit is an attractive striped red with snow white flesh which is crisp and fine textured. The trees grow vigorously and produce quantities of fine fruit.

Lodi — For years Yellow Transparent was the leading early apple, but with the introduction of the new Early Golden Lodi, it has faded into the background. Lodi is a large, quick-bearing, blight resistant improvement over Yellow Transparent, which was originated by the New York Experiment Station. Fruits are much larger and ripen almost as early as Yellow Transparent. The trees bear younger, have a better flavour and do not get mealy and soft as do those of Yellow Transparent. The sprightly rich flavour makes it a great kitchen favourite. Also when fully ripe, it attains a pleasantly mild flavour and is really good to eat. Fruits are large, uniform and round. Stems are long and thick. Colour is a most attractive, vivid yellow, which occasionally has a slight blush on the exposed cheek. Flesh is white, firm, tender, juicy, sub-acid, attaining a mild aromatic flavour. Lodi is fast becoming one of the most popular early new Summer apples for home, local and roadside orchards. You will find it available in both standard and dwarf trees. The children will thank you each year for planting this variety for early eating apples.

A.

B.

C.

D.

Courtesy of Kelly Bros., Dansville, N.Y.

A. **Wealthy**
B. **Yellow Delicious**
C. **Red Macintosh**
D. **Early Macintosh**

Early MacIntosh — Don't confuse this with the regular Winter MacIntosh. However it resembles its MacIntosh parent with its handsome red colour and uniform round shape. For the home orchard or commercial use this is an ideal early variety to plant. Trees are vigorous growers, hardy and productive. It tends to bear fruit every other year, although early thinning will often force the trees to fruit annually. Early MacIntosh comes into bearing at an early age, and the flesh is white, tender and juicy with a fine flavour.

Wealthy — This variety of apple undoubtedly has the best quality of all the Summer apples. Fruits are very beautiful, moderate in size and coloured a brilliant red. Wealthy trees are extremely hardy and can be widely planted in cold climates. The trees start to produce apples at a very early age, and bear heavily. Juice is refreshing and wine-like. Wealthy apples are excellent cookers and make extremely good eating.

Yellow or Golden Delicious is without a doubt the best yellow apple in the world. On dwarf trees, big luscious golden apples

Courtesy of Stark Bros., Louisiana, Missouri

Golden Delicious — world's youngest bearing Apple

Courtesy of Stark Bros., Louisiana, Missouri

Stark EarliBlaze — a new highly colored summer apple with extra good quality

are often produced the first year after planting. Colour is a glowing sunny yellow, sometimes blushed with rose. Fruits are extra large and often measure 4 inches or more in diameter. The flavour is sweet and delicious touched with a faint trace of spicy acidity. In areas close to Chicago and Detroit the fruit is ready for picking early in October. It is always a good, solid, crisp, juicy late keeper. Makes fine apple sauce and mouth-watering pies, and is one of the best apples for eating.

Red Delicious is one of the most popular apples grown today, either in the home garden or in commercial orchards. It is an extra large apple, fine solid red in colour, with cream-coloured flesh. There have been

individual fruits of this variety which measured $4\frac{1}{2}$ inches in length and 4 inches in diameter. It will be ready for picking about the first of October in most areas adjacent to Chicago and Detroit. Red Delicious has fine keeping qualities, and stays crisp and juicy until the beginning of Spring. It is acclaimed everywhere as one of the very best eating apples, owing to its very mild and almost sweet flavour. Trees grow vigorously, producing quantities of fruit at an early age. The hardiness of the Red Delicious has never been questioned.

Cortland is a cross between MacIntosh and Ben Davis, and exhibits the best qualities of both. It's a good dessert apple maturing later than MacIntosh. Trees are strong

McIntosh is one of the top rated apples of the past 100 years

growers and very hardy. Fruits are red, extra large and round. Cortland apples are always excellent keepers.

MacIntosh Red has been one of the top rated and most popular apples ever since it was found growing in Eastern Ontario almost a century ago. This is a tender, juicy, winter apple with a peculiar fragrance that makes it popular everywhere. Colour is a beautiful crimson red and the flesh is

crisp, delicate and almost snow white. Trees are extremely long lived, very hardy, strong spreading growers which come into bearing when they are very young. Fruits are large and very juicy, the trees being annual and prolific bearers. The apples are excellent for eating, cooking, drying and for making cider.

Northern Spy — For after-Christmas eating, there is no apple to touch the dis-

**Apples are usually planted in the early Spring,
but in temperate climates can also be planted in the Fall**

tinctive and pleasing flavour of a Northern Spy apple. Flesh is crisp, firm, juicy, and the fruits are equally good for eating or cooking. The apples are large in size and solid red in colour. The trees are extremely hardy, long lived, vigorous and very productive. In addition to being excellent eating and cooking apples, they also make first-class cider.

Rhode Island Greening is unsurpassed

as a cooking apple and also is very good for eating. It's a good keeper, but keeps better if picked early. This Greening is a beautiful yellow colour when ripe and bears heavy crops which start when the trees are very young.

Dolgo Crab Apple — Crab apple jelly is a favourite with nearly everyone and the Dolgo Crab Apple produces masses of bright red fruit which are unsurpassed for

Courtesy of A. B. Morse Co.

**Not all Crab Apples produce edible fruits,
but the Dolgo Crab is noted for its fine flavored fruits**

Beware of the bulldozer

jelly. Most housewives agree that the fruits of this Crab Apple will produce perfect jellies even when over-ripe. The Dolgo crab apple is worth planting in any garden just for the masses of beautiful bloom which are produced late in May, and thickly cover the branches. The fruits are not only good for making jelly, but also can be canned whole, made into a sauce, or pickled. Trees are extremely hardy and start to produce regular crops of crab apples when very young.

Courtesy of Stark Bros., Louisiana, Missouri

New Starkrimson Apple — acclaimed the best of all the Red Delicious Apples

Stark Florence Crab is another extremely valuable red variety of crab apple. Trees are heavy producers of crimson red crab apples of good size, which are unexcelled for jelly, preserves, jams and pickles. You will find the trees dwarf in size, and together with the pink blooms and ruby red fruits, they make one of the best trees for ornamental planting in the lawn. Some trees have been known to produce half a bushel of fruit when only two years old.

Starkrimson Delicious Apple—Fruit growers and horticulturists all over the United States and Canada are singing the praises of the new *Starkrimson Delicious Apple*. This is the apple tree for the home gardener to plant because it's a natural semi-dwarf which reaches two thirds the size of a standard apple tree in growth and won't overrun the average sized garden. The smaller stature of the tree is a boon to gardeners as it facilitates pruning.

Starkrimson is the newest member of the world famous Stark Delicious Apple family which had its beginning in 1895 when the original Stark Delicious brought the world a new flavour standard in apples. Later the now famous and widely planted Golden Delicious and Starking Delicious were introduced.

One of the world's largest apple growers has said that it is a great apple on a great tree and that it produces fruit in eighteen months. He also hints that it could revolutionize the apple industry, as it simplifies so many growing problems.

A horticulturist expert is on record as having praised its quality and colour, its attractiveness (making it easier to sell) and its characteristic of attaining its high colour early, thus enabling it to be picked while juicy and crisp.

Why is Starkrimson so different to other apples? First of all, its colour is a brilliant

A dwarf or semi-dwarf Apple Tree is best for the home garden.

Courtesy of A. B. Morse Co.

Courtesy of A. B. Morse Co.

An Apple can be used as a lawn specimen tree

glossy red which on the usual Delicious harvesting date grades 100 percent Extra Fancy for colour.

Secondly, it's a Fruit-Spur Type tree producing fruit-bearing spurs which cover the limbs down to and sometimes even on the trunk.

Most fruits on regular apple trees are borne on fruit spurs which are short, fat growth along the limbs of bearing age trees. Starkrimson has a completely different habit of growth from regular trees. The main difference is the more abundant production of strong fruit spurs which are well distributed throughout the trees. The fruit spurs are blunt, not sharp. All fruit spur buds are round and fat as contrasted to the long, sharp leaf buds. The fruit spurs

form at a much younger age than on any other type of apple tree. This brings Starkrimson into younger and heavier production and also gives better annual bearing, since there are always a number of spurs resting during each growing season to produce next year's crop.

Tests in many sections of North America have proved that Starkrimson and other spur-type apples are considerably hardier in bloom than other types of Delicious apples. In addition the spur-type growth matures earlier in the Fall and has stocky thick twigs so it's not subject to early freezing like many others.

Because it starts bearing the second or third year after planting, Starkrimson will produce twice as much during the first ten

Bartlett Pear

Courtesy of Kelly Bros., Dansville, N.Y.

years as the present Delicious strains. Apples are of uniform size and true Delicious shape.

Starkrimson is also available in dwarf spur-type trees which are ideal for city lots and home fruit gardens.

Whether you plant the dwarf or the regular Starkrimson type *you'll need to plant another variety of apples close by for pollination purposes.*

Apples and nuts grown in your own garden add beauty to the Christmas table setting

Courtesy of Stark Bros., Louisiana, Missouri

Courtesy of A. B. Morse Co.

A dwarf Pear Tree is the best kind to plant in a small garden

Seckel

Bosc

Dymond

Clapp's Favorite

Courtesy of Kelly Bros., Dansville, N.Y.

PEAR TREES

Recommended varieties of Pears

Bartlett — There is not the slightest doubt that the Bartlett is North America's favourite pear for size and taste. There is hardly a person who doesn't know the Bartlett pear and its qualities. It is grown in, and is adaptable to, many different climates, soils and situations. The fruits of the Bartlett are recognized as being the fanciest and the finest of all pears. Fruits are large, pyramidal in shape and golden yellow in colour with a reddish blush on the sunny side. Flesh is tender, fine grained, buttery, rich and juicy and possesses a delicious musky aroma. Trees are vigorous, grow to a large size, start to bear young and live for many years. Barring frost during blossom time, they'll bear full crops year after year.

Max Red Bartlett — As mentioned above, everyone knows the Bartlett pear, but now we have a newer, special Bartlett pear which features solid bright red colouring. Otherwise, it's almost the same as

Bartlett but has a richer, more mellow, true Bartlett flavour. The trees bear young and heavily. It is such a fine pear your friends will exclaim with delight when they see the mahogany red colour of the ripened fruit.

Beurre Bosc — Here is a very popular pear which has wonderful keeping qualities. A pear which is rated by all as "very good", or by some as "best". It has a long tapering neck and a long stem which allows it to sway in heavy winds without dropping. Colour is a brownish yellow and the flesh is tender, buttery, very juicy, with a rich flavour and pleasing aroma. Bosc has a reputation for being an excellent pollinator and makes an excellent variety for planting with other trees such as the Bartlett and Clapp's Favourite. The trees are slow growers, but they're more productive. You

Pear trees can be grown espalier style up the side of a wall just like a grapevine.

Courtesy of A. B. Morse Co.

Burbank Grand Prize Prune is one of the largest and best textured

will find the Bosc to be a most delicious eating pear.

Clapp's Favourite — This is a large yellow full-bodied favourite which thrives where other varieties of pears fail. The fruits resemble Bartlett in size and shape and ripen about the middle of August. They hang like golden pendants, inviting you to reach out and bite into the superbly flavoured, fine textured, white, juicy flesh.

The trees grow strong and sturdy producing an abundance of delicious fruit every year. This variety of pears is extremely hardy.

Dymond — It has been said that the Dymond is the perfect pear, combining the best qualities of the other varieties. It starts out with large white blossoms in early May, and produces mature fruit in early September. Extra large, superbly flavoured pears with a scarlet blush, invite you to taste

Courtesy of Kelly Bros., Dansville, N.Y.

Collette Everbearing pear

them. Dymond stands straight, is resistant to disease, is self-pollinizing and can be depended upon to produce a bountiful crop of fruit year after year. This is a distinct new variety that is vigorous, hardy and outstanding in every regard.

Collette Pear is one of the most amazing new fruits we have seen. It is everbearing from early Fall to freeze up, and in addition is one of the most delicious pears on the market. Fruits are firm, juicy, and sweet, and do not rot at the core when ripe. Collette pears are ideal for canning and we guarantee you have never tasted a better pear. Fruits are large and smooth textured and will truly surprise your friends and neighbours.

Burbank Giant Yellow Plum, earliest of all yellow freestone plums

Courtesy of Stark Bros., Louisiana, Missouri

PLUMS AND PRUNE TREES

Stanley Plum

Courtesy of Kelly Bros., Dansville, N.Y.

Courtesy of Kelly Bros., Dansville, N.Y.

Shiro Plum

Burbank Mammoth Cardinal — a wonderful yellow fleshed plum

Courtesy of Stark Bros., Louisiana, Missouri

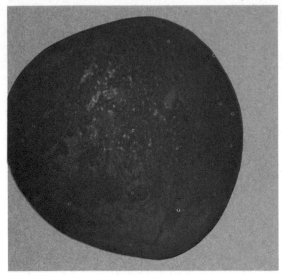

Santa Rosa

Plums and Prune trees — Plum and prune trees usually start to bear the second or third year after planting, depending on the care they receive and the growth that they make. Distance to plant apart is 20 feet.

With the exception of the prunes of the German and Stanley varieties which are self pollinating, plums need to be interplanted to ensure bearing fruit. Should you decide to plant plum trees, make sure you use European varieties for pollinating that class, and Oriental kinds for those varieties. Burbank and Santa Rosa are typical Oriental varieties. Reine Claude and Lombard are representative European kinds.

Burbank Red Ace Plum

Stark Giant Damson Plum makes delicious jams, jellies and preserves

Recommended varieties of
Plums and Prunes

Early Golden is a new Canadian plum which originated at Fonthill, Ontario. It has rapidly become a favourite because of its earliness and golden yellow colour that has a faint reddish blush when matured. The plums are free-stone and have good firm flesh. Trees are heavy croppers, and grow very vigorously. This is the first plum to ripen, and the trees are extremely hardy.

Lombard—Here we have an old favourite plum which is attaining new popularity, especially in the home garden. There is no better plum for making jam or for eating. Its colour is light to dark purplish red with thick bloom. Flesh is yellow in colour, juicy, firm and sweet. Stones are semi-free to free. Fruits ripen around the first of September, are oval in shape and of medium to large size. Trees grow 12 to 15 feet tall, have a round top and are hardy and

Courtesy of Ontario Agricultural College

Trees give a garden a finished look

greenish-yellow in colour, will be marked with red if the fruit is thinned and sufficiently exposed to the sun. Trees grow only moderately high, usually about 12 to 15 feet. Plums are usually ripe between the 25th and the 30th of September. They have a luscious eating and canning quality, considered to be the standard of excellence.

Bradshaw is a very large and fine early plum. The fruits have an attractive dark violet skin with contrasting yellow flesh. They are very juicy and excellent for eating and canning. Trees grow vigorously and are very hardy. The Bradshaw plum has the ability to produce heavy crops of delicious fruit every year. Ripening time is September 5th to the 10th.

very productive.

Reine Claude — This is also known as Greengage and is one of the most popular of all plums. The beautiful fruit, large, pale

Flowering crab apples come in many varieties and colors

Courtesy of A. B. Morse Co.

Burbank Plum

Courtesy of Kelly Bros., Dansville, N.Y.

Trees have moderate growth and crop well. Prunes start to ripen around the 24th to the 27th of September.

Oriental varieties of Plums

Shiro is the golden yellow plum that everyone loves to see and eat. The low-growing hardy trees bear immense crops every year. Fruits have exceptional high quality, are very tender and juicy. The Shiro is in a class by itself for eating purposes, and it also has good cooking quality, but unfortunately for this purpose it is not free-stone. Plums will be ready for picking between August 8th and the 15th.

Superior — This plum is exceptionally hardy and is recommended for the Northern and Western States. Fruits are free-stone, sweet and juicy. The yellow flesh is covered with wine-red skin. Plant two trees for best results, or if planted singly, is a good pollinizer for other plums. Fruits become ripe early in August.

Prune type Plums

Stanley is an exceptionally productive variety introduced at the New York State Experimental Station. Many garden experts consider it the best prune for home use and commercial planting. Among its better qualities is the fact that it bears fruit in just three years, and ripens ten days earlier than other varieties. The large, deep bluish-purple fruits are firm and sweet and have a very excellent flavour.

Fellenberg (also known as Italian and German) — This is a widely known and valuable plum for dessert, but most of its reputation is in drying for preserves. Fruits are long, oval, and purple in colour with a thick bloom. Flesh is firm, sweet and pleasant and separates freely from the stone.

Santa Rosa — No garden is complete without this very promising Oriental variety of plum. Fruits are extremely large, handsome, and dark red in colour with purple overtones. Flesh is very juicy, of good quality and has an attractive red colour. Trees are large, vigorous, and moderately productive. Plums are ripe anytime during the last ten days of August.

Burbank — This is a variety that has been on the market for a considerable time, and yet loses none of its popularity with the passing years. Fruits are very large, especially if thinning is carried out. The best time to thin out is when the plums are small and green, this enhances the colour and quality. Colour is a bright red with some purple overtones. Flesh is meaty and quite firm. Fruits should be picked before they are entirely ripe.

The low growing trees are flat topped, with somewhat drooping branches which make them attractive in the garden from the time they start to flower until the leaves drop in late Fall. There are few varieties of plums which are more productive. Fruits will be ripe during the last week in August.

Flowering crab apples are one of the hardiest of the flowering trees

Plum trees for much below zero districts—These plums have been developed mostly at the Morden Experimental Station in Manitoba, especially for the VERY COLD DISTRICTS. The fruits, of course are never as large as the varities that are grown in the warmer areas, but are nevertheless just as acceptable.

Assiniboine — Fruits are bright red,

have a yellowish flesh, are quite juicy and of very good quality. They start to ripen about the middle of August. This variety is an excellent pollinizer.

Mount Royal — The trees produce large blue fruits of excellent quality. Flesh is yellow, firm, juicy, sweet and the quality is quite good. Ripening time is the middle of September. This is one of the very har-

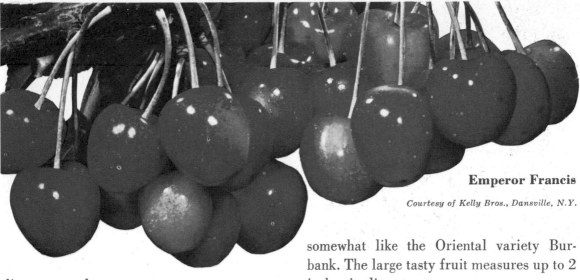

Emperor Francis

Courtesy of Kelly Bros., Dansville, N.Y.

diest prune plums.

Grenville — Here we have a very high yielding plum whose bright red colour is somewhat like the Oriental variety Burbank. The large tasty fruit measures up to 2 inches in diameter.

Underwood — Trees of Underwood are medium in size and they produce large

Schmidts Biggareau is one of the best black sweet cherries

Courtesy of Stark Bros., Louisiana, Missouri

Courtesy of Kelly Bros., Dansville, N.Y.

**Black Tartarian is the earliest of
all sweet cherries**

round fruits whose colour is yellow, over-laid with light to rich red, combined with a faint waxy bloom. Flesh is golden yellow, tender, juicy, sweet and the quality excellent. Fruiting season is the third week in August.

CHERRIES

Sweet cherries start to bear the third or fourth year after planting. The trees may be planted as close as 25 feet apart. Sweet cherries are not self-pollinating, or the technical name, self unfruitful, and so must be inter-planted with other varieties. Where Napoleon and Emperor Francis are to be planted together, another variety such as

Van Sweet Cherry is a new super-hardy cherry which ripens in mid-season

Courtesy of Stark Bros., Louisiana, Missouri

Montmorency

Windsor is one of the best of the dark sweet cherries

Windsor or Black Tartarian must be added, as the first two will not pollinate each other.

Sour cherries begin to bear the second or third year after planting, and should be set 20 feet apart. Sour cherries are self-fruitful, but they will not pollinate sweet cherries, and vice versa.

Black Tartarian is the earliest of all the sweet cherries. This well-known and popular cherry produces very large, bright purplish-black fruits which are juicy and have a rich flavour. Black Tartarian cherries are excellent for canning. Trees are remarkably vigorous and erect growers, and will produce immense crops. Does well on a wide range of soils. Ripening date for Black Tartarian is any time between June 20th and July 4th, depending on your climatic location. One of the big problems with Black Tartarians is the attacks of birds on the cherries. This is mainly because it's the first variety to ripen, and the birds, particularly robins, seem to want to get their fill on the first cherries of the season. Light netting covering the tree and branches seems to be the only satisfactory way of protecting the cherries from the birds.

Emperor Francis is recognized as one of the newer leading sweet cherries for home and commercial orchards. This high quality cherry resembles Napoleon in size and colour, except that its colour is a little darker. You can start to pick the fruit around July 4th.

Napoleon or Royal Ann — Here is a choice sweet cherry which is good for canning and eating. Cherries are large size, pale yellow with a bright red cheek, sweet, juicy and firm. Ripening date is anywhere from July 7th to the 10th.

Windsor — This is one of the best quality dark cherries, and is often referred to as Black Oxheart. It has long been regarded as the main sweet cherry variety. Fruits are large and dark red in colour, almost black, and are sweet, firm and rich. They're delicious to eat fresh and wonderful for canning. The trees grow upright and are rapid and vigorous growers. It's probably as hardy as any sweet cherry, and the ripening date is from July 20th to 26th.

Schmidt's Bigarreau — It would be

Courtesy of Kelly Bros., Dansville, N.Y.

**North Star Dwarf Cherry is the variety
to grow where the climate is cold**

hard to find a larger variety of sweet cherries. Fruits are produced in clusters and they have a very fine black colour if allowed to remain on the trees until the correct picking time. They are very delicious to eat either fresh or canned, and keep well. Picking time is around the 10th to 12th of July.

Empress Eugenie — Here is a variety of sweet cherry that has been found to be more hardy than any other. It has proven to be hardy even during very cold years when the temperature has dipped as low as 10° below zero. For the home gardener this is a good variety because the tree doesn't ripen all at the one time, but does so gradually, and ripe cherries may be picked over a much longer period of time. Fruits are dark red in colour, tender, meaty, and have a pleasing tart flavour.

Fruit of the North Star Cherry

Sour Cherries — Montmorency — There is not the slightest doubt in the world that Montmorency is the best red sour cherry. These large, dark red, very firm, fine flavoured cherries are much sought after by the housewife for pies, canning and jam purposes. This is the cherry that the canning factories buy by the hundreds of tons. Trees are very hardy, standing below zero temperatures and come into bearing the second or third year after planting. Sour cherries as well as sweet cherries need a well-drained location. If your soil is the slightest bit on the wet side, don't plant cherries. On the other hand, if your soil is stony or gravelly, you can expect much success from cherries. The fruits of Montmorency start to ripen in early to mid-July, and the blossoms are self fertilizing.

Dwarf Cherry

North Star— This is the cherry to grow in areas where the climate is very cold. North Star is an amazing dwarf tree, growing only 5 to 7 feet high. Cherries are produced by the thousands, having tender flesh which is juicy and meaty. Colour is bright red, changing to a deep mahogany red. Fruit starts to ripen anywhere from July 15th to the first week in August, depending upon where you live. Excellent for pies and sauce, the fruits have small stones and hang well on the tree. This dwarf cherry is a lovely tree for the garden or border whether in flower or in fruit. It generally bears the first year after planting.

PEACHES

Courtesy of Kelly Bros., Dansville, N.Y.

Nothing like picking your own peaches from the tree

Hale Haven

These are the fastest growing of all the fruit trees, and they often start to bear the second year after planting. In the home garden they are not only the most useful because of their delicious fruits, but are a real addition to the landscape, especially

Dwarf Early Elberta Peach

Courtesy of Stark Bros., Louisiana, Missouri

when covered with glorious pink blossoms in early May. Normal planting distance is 20 feet apart.

Peaches are not reliably hardy where the temperature regularly falls to 10° below zero F., during the Winter. At around 10° below zero the peach buds are killed and below 20° the trees are often killed, especially those not planted in a well drained location. It's a good idea to check with your local nurseryman or government experi-mental station to see if the climate in your area is suitable for growing peaches.

Recommended varieties of Peaches

Red Haven is rapidly becoming the leading, top quality, early peach. It's not only a very early bearer, but also a very productive one. The fruit has a most attractive bright red colour, with an orange background. Peaches are firm, of high quality and have a very delicious taste. Being a

A Peach tree is one of the better fruits to plant in the home garden

Courtesy of A. B. Morse Co.

Courtesy of Stark Bros., Louisiana, Missouri

Stark Early Elberta Peach makes fine eating

Courtesy of Stark Bros., Louisiana, Missouri

Stark EarliGlo Peach — first high quality yellow freestone peach to ripen

free-stone peach, it is also good for canning, as well as eating. You will be picking the fruits any time between August 10th and 15th. Like other peaches, Red Haven usually starts to bear the third year after planting, and you will need to plant at least one other variety with it for cross pollination purposes.

Peaches are one of the world's most popular fruits

Courtesy of The Ontario Peach Growers Assoc.

Pink blossoms of the peaches are most attractive

Courtesy of The Ontario Peach Growers Assoc.

Courtesy of Stark Bros., Louisiana, Missouri

Peaches start to bear soon after planting

Golden Jubilee — This has been one of the very best peaches ever developed, both for the home garden and for commercial orchards. It's an early yellow, free-stone peach of exceptional quality. The fruits have a red blush on the sunny side. There are more Golden Jubilee peach trees now planted than all the other varieties. It's hard to beat either for eating or canning, having fruits which are very long and oblong in shape with a delicious flavour.

Hale-Haven is a marvellous peach resulting from the crossing of the famous J. H. Hale with South Haven. The trees produce large, beautifully coloured yellow-fleshed peaches, which ripen approximately ten days to two weeks ahead of Elberta.

Peaches are perfectly free-stone and are of the highest quality. Trees are strong growers and heavy bearers. Peaches start to ripen during the first week in September.

J. H. Hale is an extra large free-stone peach whose flesh is golden yellow and is delicious in flavour. It must be cross-pollinized with some other variety in order to ensure a crop of peaches. The usual ripening date is between September 17th and 21st.

Fowler — This peach was developed by Mr. George R. Fowler of Marlboro, N.Y. It's a large yellow peach of the Elberta type and is extremely hardy. Trees are vigorous growers, and exceptionally disease resistant.

The new Red Leaf Peach

Fruit matures a week later than Elberta and ripens evenly. Peaches are firm, thick skinned and practically fuzzless.

Elberta — This has long been recognized as the best canning peach, is one of the most popular of all peaches, and you will find it planted wherever peaches are grown. Fruits are large, handsome and of high quality. It must be admitted that it is not quite as good an eating peach as Golden Jubilee or Red Haven. Fruits are ready for picking between September 10th and the 20th.

Red Leaf Peach — Here is a special new peach supplying both foliage and fruit of novelty type. The foliage is bright,

Children and cherries go well together

Courtesy of Stark Bros., Louisiana, Missouri

Just imagine having these Early Elberta Peaches growing in your garden

Courtesy of Stark Bros., Louisiana, Missouri

"J. H. Hale" — one of the best mid-season yellow freestone peaches

bronzy red during early Spring and Summer, which gradually changes to maroon in the Fall. The deep rose blossoms contrast delightfully with the colourful foliage. Fruits are also red, with golden markings, are of high quality and good flavour. This sensational tree grows 12 to 15 feet high at maturity, and produces a full crop of perfectly formed, round peaches about 1½ inches across.

Summerlong — This is a sensational new "ever-bearing" peach. Fruits are produced from late July to about September 15th and are medium in size, yellow, freestone and of excellent quality. The flesh is sweet and tasty, and does not bruise easily. Fruit and blossoms appear on the tree at the same time. The long bearing season allows you to pick fruit for two whole months instead of just a few weeks.

APRICOTS

Courtesy of Kelly Bros., Dansville, N.Y.

An example of fine Apricots

Most home gardeners are not aware that apricots can be grown even in the really cold areas. There are varieties on the market now which will withstand temperatures as much as 30° to 40° below zero, and still produce delicious fruit. Apricots are valuable both for their fruits and as a beautiful ornamental flowering shade tree. It's always necessary to plant two varieties to ensure cross pollination.

Perfection is an outstanding variety with fruits of a rich golden apricot colour, having exceptional size and delicious fla-

Wilson Delicious Apricot is extra hardy

Courtesy of Stark Bros., Louisiana, Missouri

Elberta Peaches are the best late flowering variety

your. The trees start to bear when very young, and are extremely hardy. The original tree at Waterville, Oregon at an elevation of 2,650 feet has withstood temperatures as low as 30° below zero, and extremely rigorous climatic conditions.

Morden No. 604 was developed at the famous Morden Experimental Farm in Manitoba, Canada. This organization specializes in developing new varieties of quality fruits which will withstand the extremely cold temperatures just north and south of the western Canada-United States border. The trees of Morden No. 604 are upright, tall, healthy and vigorous. Fruits are large, medium golden-yellow in colour which be-

comes darker and reddish when fully ripe. The flesh has a bright orange-red colour, is firm and sweet, and of good quality. The skin is tender and cooking tests at Morden, place this new variety right at the top.

Moorpark is a most attractive apricot with high quality and fine flavour. Fruit is large, deep yellow with a red cheek. The trees grow about the same size as a peach tree and ripen in mid-August.

Early Golden is a new free-stone apricot which posseses a very fine flavour. Skin is smooth, fuzzless and a pale orange in colour. Fruits are medium to large in size and make very good eating.

Dwarf Fruit Tree

Dwarf Plums

These are all courtesy of
Kelly Bros., Dansville, N.Y.

Yellow Delicious

DWARF FRUIT TREES FOR THE HOME GARDEN

Delightful Spring blossoms, Summer shade and delicious fruits in the Fall, are the triple values offered by planting fruit trees in the garden. For the beginner to gardening and for the average small garden, the best plan is to plant dwarf fruit trees.

It's true that a dwarf fruit tree will not bear as much fruit as a standard tree, but this can be remedied by planting more trees in the same space, and in the end you will have about the same quantity of fruit. Even our commercial fruit growers have begun to

recognize this fact, and many of them are switching to dwarf or semi-dwarf trees. On the other hand, for the home owner who has the space and wants shade as well as blossoms and fruits, the standard size trees may be preferred.

Certainly dwarf trees will bear very much earlier, usually starting a year after planting. The crop will get larger as the tree grows older. Most standard size trees will take a minimum of 5 years before they bear fruit. Standard size Northern Spy Apples

Dwarf Apple trees such as "Jonathan" are now grown on their own root stock

can take as long as 10 years before starting to produce apples.

Up to the moment the only fruit trees that have been successfully dwarfed are apples and pears. Peaches and sour cherries can be kept to a small size by heavy pruning.

The same pollination problem is common to both dwarf and standard fruit trees. You need at least two different varieties of apples or pears for pollination purposes. Apples will not pollinate pears.

Dwarf fruit trees must always be staked at planting time unless you intend to train them along a fence or a wall in what is called "Espalier" fashion like a grape vine or making the trees grow in a bush form. Staking is done for three reasons, to

strengthen the union or graft, to carry the crop of fruit which is generally heavy compared to the size of the trees, and to prevent breakage of the rather brittle roots.

Nurserymen have to do much more work in producing dwarfs than in growing standard trees. The main method is to bud or graft a standard variety of apple or pear to the root of a small-growing variety. In this respect root stock have been investigated more thoroughly for apples than for pears and other fruits. The East Malling Fruit Research Station in England has done outstanding work in this field. They have developed a series of root stocks giving different degrees of dwarfing for apples. The rootstocks are classified as full dwarfing for those that produce very small trees, semi-dwarfing for those that develop trees intermediate in size between the full dwarf and the standard trees.

Pear trees are dwarfed by using quince stock. Some varieties, including the popular Bartlett, do not unite well with quince. In such cases a compatible variety such as Beurre Hardy is first budded on the quince. The desired variety is then budded to Beurre Hardy. Trees about half the size of the standard pear trees are produced.

It's very important when planting the dwarf trees to make sure the bud or graft is 3 to 4 inches above the level of the soil. You can easily locate the point where the graft or the bud was made by finding the bulge

Clapp's Favorite

Courtesy of Kelly Bros., Dansville, N.Y.

Dwarf Apple trees bear fruit from the ground up

Courtesy of Stark Bros., Louisiana, Missouri

For the small garden a dwarf flowering crab apple is an excellent lawn speciment

on the trunk a few inches above the roots. If you allow the point where the tree was grafted or budded to come in contact with the soil the odds are the tree will no longer be dwarf. Remember that above the bud or graft the tree is just the same as any standard variety and if this part of the tree starts to produce roots then you no longer have a dwarf tree.

For most gardens the fully dwarf trees are the best. Place full-dwarf apples 10 to 12 feet apart each way. Set the semi-dwarf trees 20 feet apart each way.

When planting dwarfs prune them back to keep the top in balance with the roots. A loss of roots always occurs in transplanting. If the trees are single stems 3 to 4 feet high, prune them back to about 30 inches. Generally no further pruning is needed during the first year.

These are all courtesy of Kelly Bros., Dansville, N.Y.

New Hardy Carpathian English Walnut

Chinese Chestnuts

NUT TREES TO GROW IN THE HOME GARDEN AND WOODLAND

Not too many home gardeners, beginners or experienced, realize that nut trees are wonderful for planting in the home garden or in woodlands. Such trees not only provide delicious nuts for the whole family, but also make attractive shade trees.

Most varieties of nut trees require the same kind of soil as would be needed to grow a good crop of vegetables. In other words, the soil should contain a quantity of plant food and humus, be well drained, and have a fair supply of moisture.

The best location for such trees would be on a warm, southern slope, the sunny side of buildings, or any sheltered spot where there is sunshine.

The time to plant is as early as possible in the Spring. You must be a good deal more careful planting a nut tree than a fruit tree or an ordinary shade tree.

Flowering Almond is a sight to behold when in bloom

Courtesy of Ontario Agricultural College

Halls Almond

Filberst (Hazelnut)

Hardy Pecan

Thomas Grafted Black Walnut

These are all courtesy of
Kelly Bros., Dansville, N.Y.

Butternuts

Whatever you do, don't leave the roots exposed to the sun and the wind. The best plan is to go out to the nursery, buy your tree, then take it home and plant it. Before you go to the nursery have the planting hole prepared.

The depth to plant will be the same depth as the tree was planted out in the nursery row. You can always recognize this by the soil line on the bark of the tree above the roots. In planting you dig a hole much larger than the spread of the roots. Also make the hole about six inches deeper than the planting depth required. Into the bottom of the hole place a handful of complete fertilizer or plant food. Then cover this with enough soil to bring to the required planting depth. As with any other tree, or shrub, you replace the soil removed from the hole with a good top soil containing about one-third either peat moss, material from the home compost heap or well-rotted barnyard manure.

You will need a stake to set into place at the same time as you start planting the tree. The stake is placed on the same side of the tree as the prevailing wind. For instance, if the prevailing wind is from the West, then place the stake at the West side of the tree. This will prevent damage to the roots later on if you try to drive a stake between the

Courtesy of Stark Bros., Louisiana, Missouri

Trees, lawns, and flowers beautify the garden

roots after planting. Hold the tree and the stake in place and spread the roots of the tree carefully out. Then add three or four inches of the good top soil mixture and firm it down by tramping with the feet. Gradually fill and firm until the hole is half filled, then fill the hole with water and let it drain away. By doing this you firm the soil around the roots and eliminate any air pockets. Gradually fill and firm the soil until the hole is full. Leave a saucer-shaped depression at the top for watering purposes. Then place a mulch of peat moss, straw, grass clippings or old hay for three or four feet out from the trunk of the tree. This will retain some of the moisture in the soil, keeping the soil and roots cool.

Recommended varieties of nut trees

Carpathian or English Walnut — One of the best nut trees to plant in the home garden is the hardy Carpathian or English Walnut. This is a fairly fast-growing tree and does best in gravelly or sandy soil. Trees have glossy dark green leaves and grow to a height of 35 to 40 feet. There is no doubt about their hardiness, because they have survived the coldest Winter on record in New York State. As far as we know there are no disease or insect problems, and so spraying is unnecessary. You will need to plant at least two trees to ensure adequate pollination and large crops of fruits.

Chinese Chestnut — In the early days

Courtesy of A. B. Morse Co.

A white flowering cherry tree puts on an exciting Spring show

of this century, a serious disease wiped out the native North American chestnut. It's a pleasure to report that we now have a new variety of sweet chestnut to take the place of those diseased some years ago. This is the Chinese chestnut which makes a fine lawn specimen tree, produces large quantities of delicious, ready-to-eat nuts, is hardy and blight resistant. The Chinese chestnut is a very fast-growing tree that flourishes in any good well-drained garden soil and soon reaches 35 feet in height. Better crops are ensured by planting two or more trees for pollination purposes.

Halls Almond — Here we have a new improved dual purpose tree. In Spring it is smothered with large pink flowers, later in September you can harvest abundant crops of delicious, tasty high quality nuts. It's a rapid growing, shapely ornamental tree with deep green foliage and quickly grows to 15 feet high. The Halls Almond is hardy and can be grown wherever it is possible to grow peach trees. Sheer beauty, restful shade and big crops of delicious nuts can be yours if you plant Halls Almond in your garden. Two trees are needed for cross pollination.

Filbert (Hazel Nut) — This fine nut tree can be grown wherever peaches flourish. The trees start to bear early and produce tasty, easy to crack nuts. It's a good tree for the home garden because it only grows 1: to 15 feet high at maturity. Larger crops o nuts are achieved when two varieties ar planted for cross pollination.